SETH PRICE

ΔΕΣΤΕ

DESTE Foundation for Contemporary Art

SETH PRICE

2000 WORDS

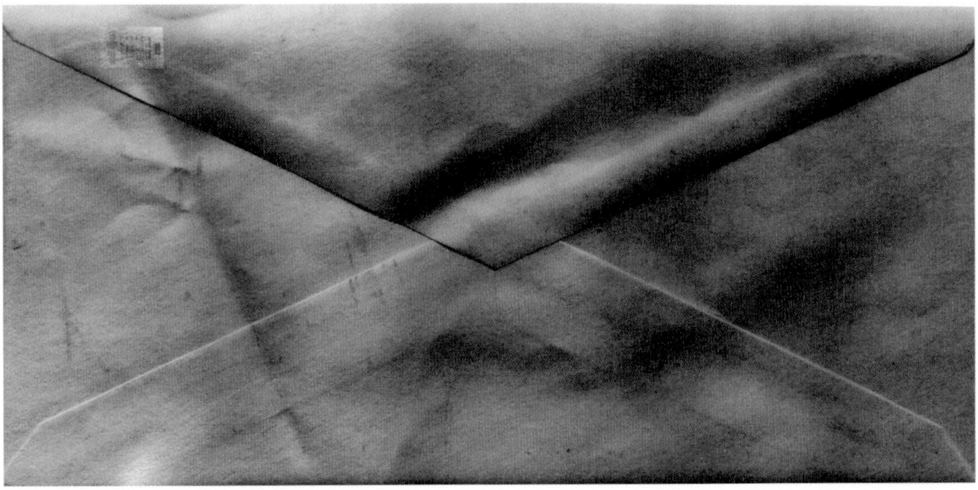

SHORT CIRCUIT

Chris Wiley

While trolling the Internet looking to dredge up everything I could about Seth Price, I found myself bounced from his main site to a separate blog with the blandly self-evident domain name sethpriceimages.com. The site is one of those image-based, infinitely unfurling affairs, where just when you think you've scrolled to the terminus, more content magically appears, lending the site the feel of an inexhaustible font of imagery and information, a kind of synecdoche of the Internet itself. It proved very helpful to my search: a vast collection of images, stretching back across the whole of Price's career, all in one convenient place. A researcher's dream! But then, an undermining kick in the ribs. Floating in the upper left corner in light gray type, invisible at first against the blog's identically colored background, hangs the flippant phrase "FUCK A CATALOG." Well, shit. Doubt bubbles to the surface: is this book necessary?

I've discovered that stumbling blocks such as this one are a common occurrence when attempting to unpack and subsequently repackage the dense storehouse of Price's work from the last decade or so, during which he has established himself as perhaps the key forerunner of a generation of artists who have imported the logic, look, and tools of the Internet age into their art. In part, this is because his work is wildly peripatetic and complex, even for our post-medium-specific age. Price has made sculptures and videos; prints and books; music, music videos, and music compilations; wall pieces made of vacuum-formed plastic, iridescent Plexiglas, and a host of other industrial materials; and has created performance pieces and even helped to design a line of clothing. Primarily, however, the difficulty in conquering these stumbling blocks lies in the fact that Price has emerged as the single most erudite interpreter of his own work, expounding on its meanings and methodologies in both his highly influential writings, and a shape-shifting artist's lecture-cum-artwork that has appeared in various permutations under the title *Redistribution* (2007–). Doubt bubbles to the surface: is this essay necessary? Fuck a catalog essay.

And yet we soldier on. But how, exactly? How do we avoid performing scripted expository pratfalls and regurgitating past shibboleths? Perhaps it is best to take a cue from Price himself, and rather than pass his works directly under the critical microscope, as he and others have done, try instead to look at them askance, to examine how he has designed them to function in the world. As a result, it might be possible to gain a better understanding not only of his work as a whole, but of his sense of where our culture is headed (or has already wound up) as a result of the massive technological upheavals that have attended the period of its production.

Not coincidentally, this approach falls in line with what is undoubtedly Price's most well-known and influential essay, *Dispersion* (2002).[1] Often misconstrued as a manifesto in the Modernist vein, the text is in fact more of a tentative proposition concerning the possibility of creating a new kind of nominally public art, one that eschews the site-specific nature of the genre in favor of creating publicness by way of a work's dispersal through channels not normally associated with artistic production, effectively hijacking these ready-made structures for artistic ends. In this way, it is part of the perennial call for the blurring of the boundaries between art and life (or art and mass media, which has staked a claim over much of life), though one that is not so much concerned with the destruction of the ivory tower of artistic autonomy, rather one that is tinged with anxiety about the possibility of art speaking at all—whether to elites or others—in an environment glutted with corporatized media of all varieties, whose techniques of circulation have all but left art in the dust.

Another stumbling block: more often than not, Price appears not to take his own advice. After all, a great majority of his work takes the form of traditional art objects and limited-edition videos, which circulate solely within the museum and gallery circuit. Even those works that hew more closely to the model outlined in *Dispersion* are limited successes in terms of proliferation, often seemingly by design.[2] How widely marketable, after all, is a compilation of mid-century academic electronic music (*'Akademische Graffiti'/'Unique Source'* [2005]), and how ready-to-wear are the high-concept clothes he made with the designer Tim Hamilton, which marry military aesthetics with latter-day Dapper Dan logo mania, only with finance giants like FDIC, PayChex, and UBS in place of Gucci, Louis Vuitton, and Fendi? What's going on here?

A stab at an answer: let's talk about packaging. Some of Price's most iconic works are his pieces in vacuum-formed plastic, which he first exhibited at Reena Spaulings Fine Art in 2004, and has continued to produce in various permutations ever since. The vacuum-forming technique was developed in the 1950s in the wake of the explosion of industrial plastics that would become a defining hallmark of that era's consumer boom. The technique is most frequently deployed in the making of packaging for all manner of consumer goods, coddling them in protective cavities molded to their contours. Price, however, has used the technique to create ghostly impressions of commonplace subject matter—faces, fists, flowers, breasts, rope, bomber jackets—packaging signifiers as if they were products. Which, of course, they are: "Image is everything."[3]

In this case, however, image is also nothing, or next to nothing. In *Redistribution*, Price comments on the generic nature of the first vacuum-formed works, saying, "It seemed like the fist and the breast were both conservative enough motifs for sculpture, they were stripped down enough that they might start to open out again. They were kind of appealingly blank."[4] This blankness, which is a kind of willed dumbness, in both senses of the word, renders the vacuum-formed pieces into something like charged voids—bristling with a suggestion of meaning, but ultimately meaningless. They are all packaging, no product.

But their packaging is itself packaged

within the structures of the art world—its white box galleries and museum spaces, its publications, its nearly unregulated flow of capital—where it is also, of course, a product. And what excellent products these packages hold: iconic, iterative, and fungible, they come in a wide array of colors and patterns, sizes and textures, begging to be bounced around the marketplace, and perhaps matched to your interior décor. There is a hilariously tongue-in-cheek caption that accompanies an image on Price's blog that depicts a work from his series of "paintings" of the backs of sealed envelopes. The piece is hanging in a collector's apartment, where it has been matched to their couch pillows; the setup buoys this reading by Price: "Nice match with the throw pillows . . . consider the colorways."[5] It is almost as if these pieces were designed for this, optimally contoured to be slotted into the packaging of the art market, in order to function as its spectral image.

Thinking this way, the aforementioned works laid out in the *Dispersion* model begin to make more sense. Each of them, in its separate way, appears to have been pointedly packaged as a reflection on its specific context: his music compilations have been released on limited-edition vinyl (for the audiophile), cassette (for the middle-aged nostalgic), and made available to stream online (for the digital native), and mirror the simultaneously fractured and fetishistic ways in which we now consume sound. *How to Disappear in America,*[6] collaged primarily from texts pulled off the Internet but sold as a hardbound book, can function almost as a joke about the redundancy of publishing in the digital age ("FUCK A CATALOG," indeed). His music videos handily ape the aesthetic of amateur Internet videos, while simultaneously pointing to their possible overlap with the work of video art pioneers like Dara Birnbaum. His fashion line is jumbled with the type of highly charged, easily read signifiers that the industry thrives on, ham-fistedly arranged according to the critical mode expected of the contemporary artist ("All-in-one ideological critique," Price has said of the collection, "too dumb to even propose."[7]).

In fact, this assiduous consideration of context even appears true of Price's texts, which interweave reasoned arguments with gnomic declarations, stock phrases ("What a time you choose to be born!" "This is the lake of our feeling," etc.), and suggestive nonsense, cannily reflecting expectations on the form and tone of quasi-academic artists' writings.[8] In their periodic obscurity (a characteristic that Price relates to poetry in a number of interviews), they also function in a fashion similar to his signature "silhouette" works, each of which is comprised of laser-cut chunks of laminated wood that, somewhat like Rubin's vase, delineate the negative space of an absent picture: the gaps are filled in by the viewer or the reader, while the definitive picture or interpretation remains elusive. Price alludes to this state of affairs in *Uptight World*, which is published in this volume for the first time, in which he (seemingly ironically) extols the virtues of "seeming" rather than "being," of the calculated, empty posture that is the essence of the "cool" as well as the "professional." Perhaps, then, everything written about Price's texts can be seen as a performative extension of the texts themselves. Doubt bubbles to the surface . . .

However, perhaps this indeterminacy in fact points toward the heart of the matter. Insofar as Price's works engage with specific contexts, or more accurately, specific distribution flows, he always takes pains to disrupt them, to pervert them, to render something about them alien, incomplete, or incomprehensible. As such, the whole of his project can perhaps be seen as a schizoid embodiment of our present, the texture of which has come to be defined less by discrete events than by the constant careening swarm of coded signifiers and mute intensities, ricocheting off one another and shifting meanings with dizzying rapidity.

Price has made comments about this state of things, and, unsurprisingly, they are contradictory. On the one hand, Price puts forward a tentatively optimistic evaluation of the digital melee: "Frenzy might in fact be homeopathic, its anxiety-producing presence a spur, although rather than encourage the articulation of meaning, it encourages existing chains of associations to fold in a strange and unanticipated way, aligning incompatible ideas and holding them in awkward proximity."[9] Indeed, the latter half of this statement could be put forward as a viable model for art in general, and Price's practice in particular. Elsewhere, however, Price is less sanguine: "Anything today that is recorded immediately becomes material that is used, reused, worked over. When the tendency is for everything to open out in all directions at all times, the problem is trying to establish a meaningful relationship between any two things. You might ask: 'Isn't that what we would all want, to endlessly open in all directions?'

But the problem is that if we can't establish a basic relation between two points, we're on the road to psychosis."[10] This negative epiphany, the loss of the thread of meaning in the winding labyrinth of endless possibility, is perhaps most potently manifested in works that engage with images of violence. For instance, *Digital Video Effect: "Holes"* (2003), makes use of grisly photos of dead bodies sourced from the Internet and the collection of works that reference or appropriate images from videos depicting Jihadist beheadings, particularly the infamous Daniel Pearl video. Unlike Thomas Hirschhorn, who makes use of such images as a means of political agitation, Price deliberately makes use of these images as a kind of raw material, useful only for their affective intensity. This could be a model for the image in the Internet age: headless, free floating, severed from meaning.

1 Seth Price, *Dispersion* (Seth Price, 2002; New York: 38th Street Publishers, 2008).

2 For example, Price's ongoing collection of compilations of obscure or extinct musical genres, *Title Variable* (2001–), which was sold in record stores and made available to stream online, or his remixed and rewritten collage of texts on dropping out of mainstream society, *How to Disappear in America* (New York: The Leopard Press, 2008), which was released in bookstores, or his series of music videos for his own electronic music, created from found footage and appropriated stills and released on Vimeo and YouTube, as well as shown in a gallery context, or the fashion line he created alongside the designer Tim Hamilton, which has been sold in high-end stores.

3 Though it has now come to be a standard quip connoting the triumph of style over substance, "Image is everything" originally achieved catchphrase status when it was suavely uttered by tennis star Andre Agassi in a 1990 advertisement for Canon's EOS Rebel camera. Further proving this statement's truth, Agassi later revealed that by the time of the ad's production, his trademark mane had begun to thin so drastically that he was forced to wear a wig.

4 Seth Price, *Redistribution* (Seth Price, 2007–).

5 Seth Price, www.sethpriceimages.com (accessed October 2013).

6 Seth Price, *How to Disappear in America* (New York: The Leopard Press, 2008).

7 Seth Price, interview by Chris Bollen, January 2012.

8 This calls to mind a conversation recounted in a lecture at the University of California, Berkeley by the analytic philosopher John Searle that took place between Searle and his friend Michel Foucault, in which Searle inquired why the eminent French thinker chose to write so poorly when his lectures were so clear and cogent. Foucault responded: "In France, you must be at least 10% incomprehensible, otherwise people won't think it's deep, they won't think you are a profound thinker." Searle claims to have later relayed this conversation to the similarly prominent French sociologist Pierre Bourdieu, who put the figure closer to 20%.

9 Seth Price, "Teen Image," *Art Fag City* (2009), http://www.artfagcity.com/2009/10/22/img-mgmt-teen-image/ (accessed January 2014).

10 Seth Price, *Redistribution*.

WORKS

Untitled Film/Right, 2006

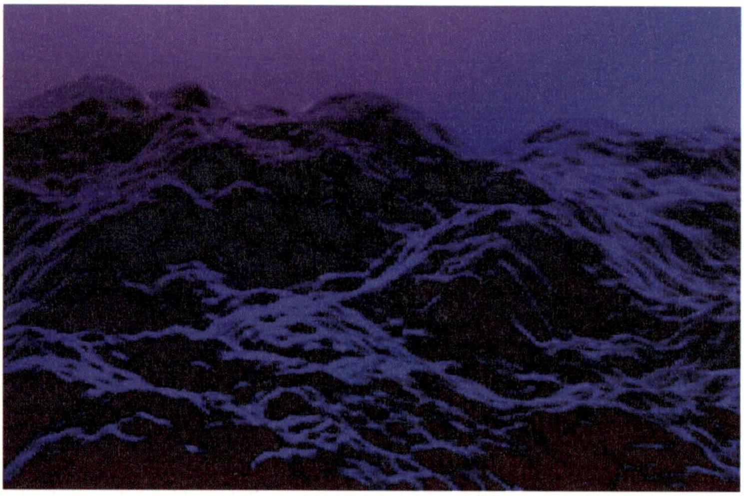

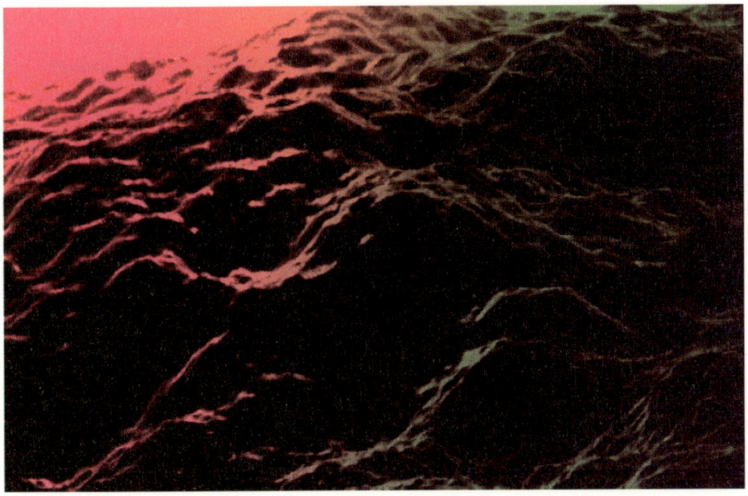

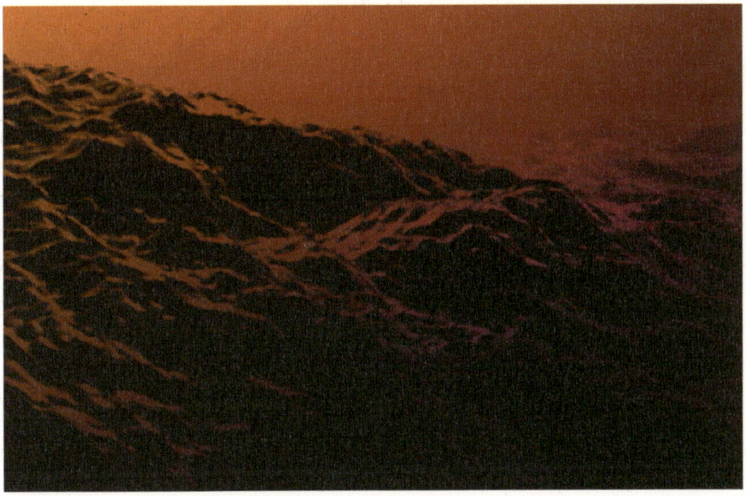

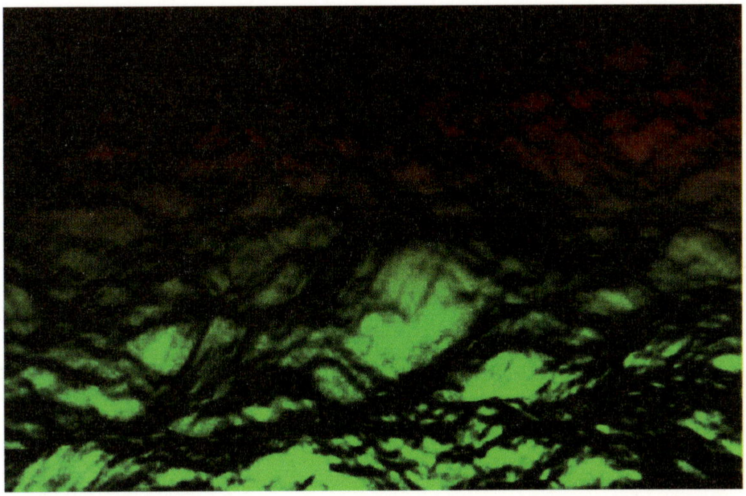

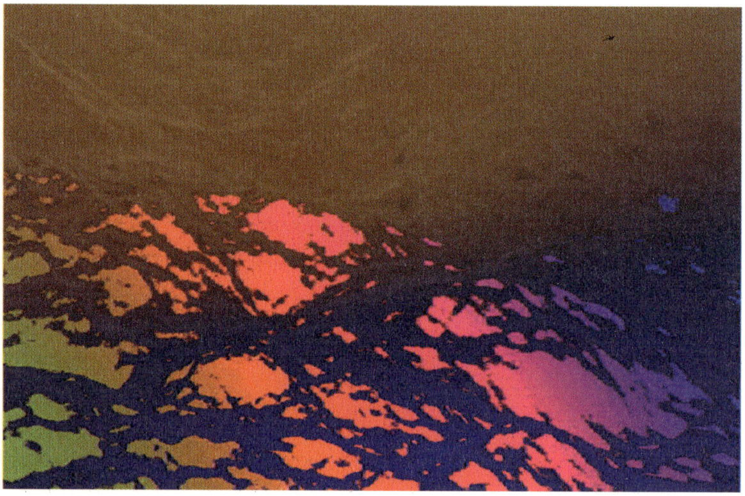

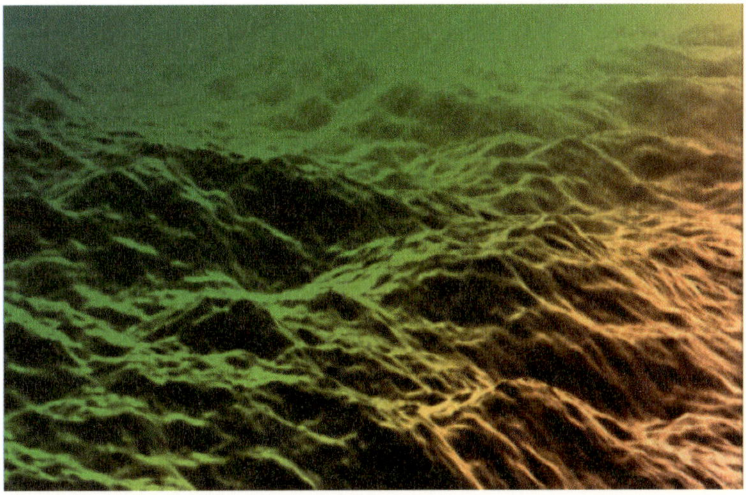

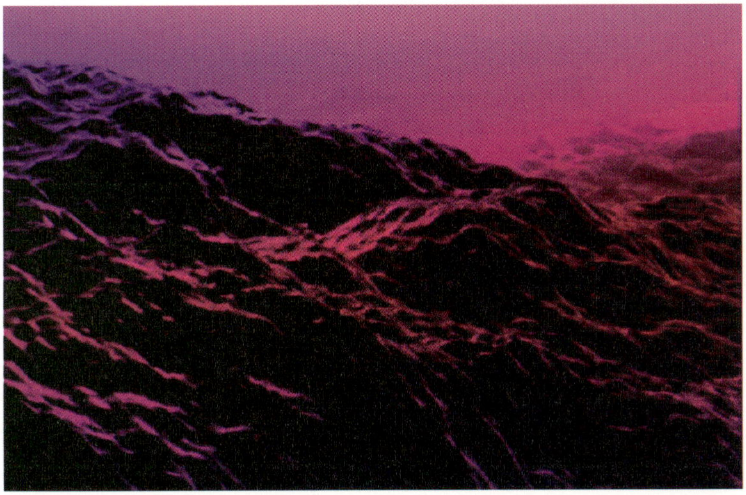

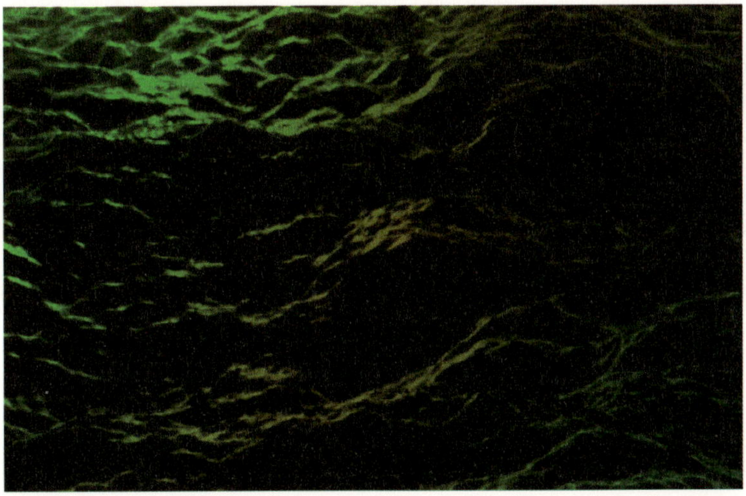

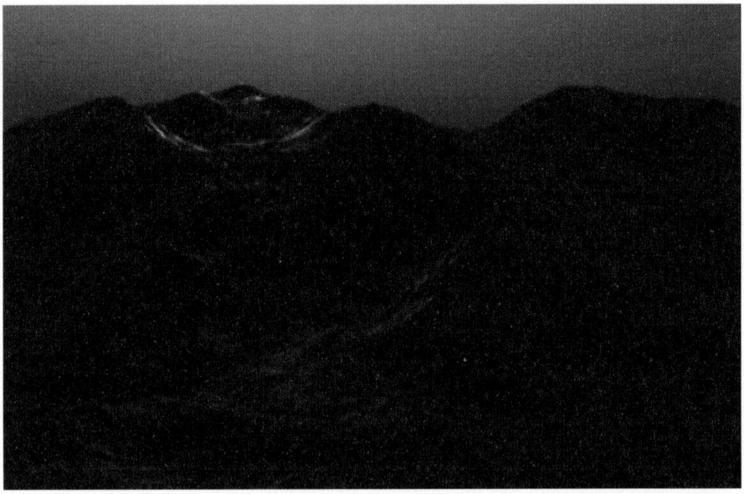

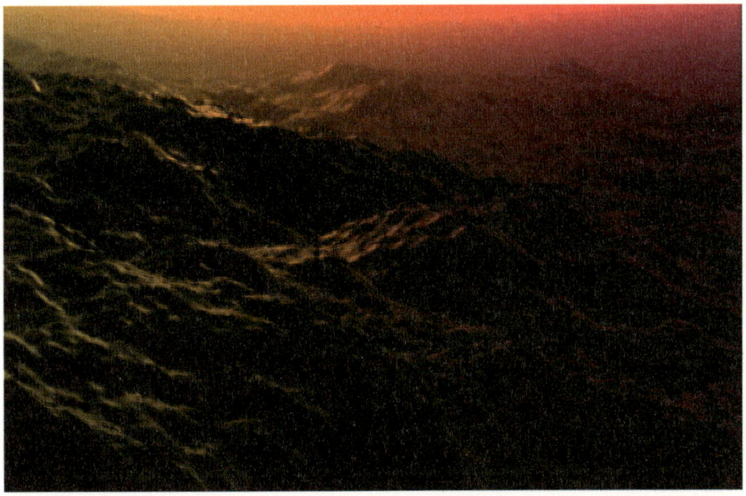

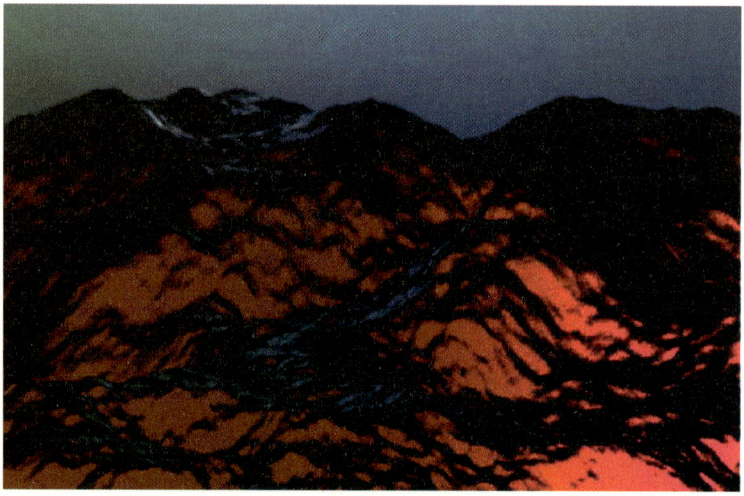

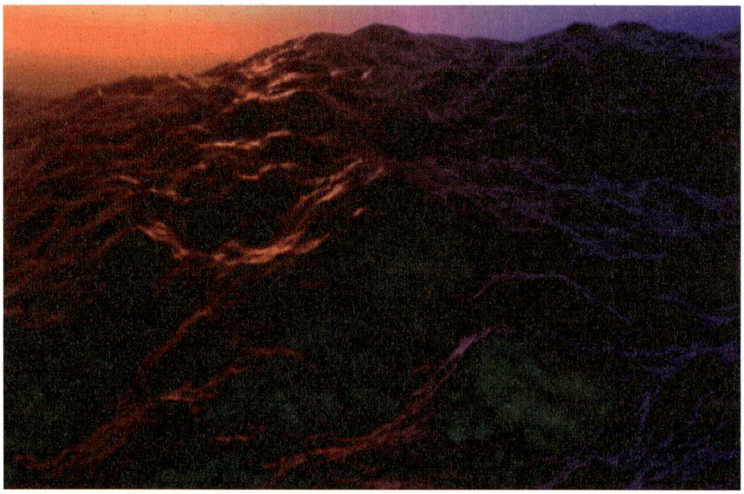

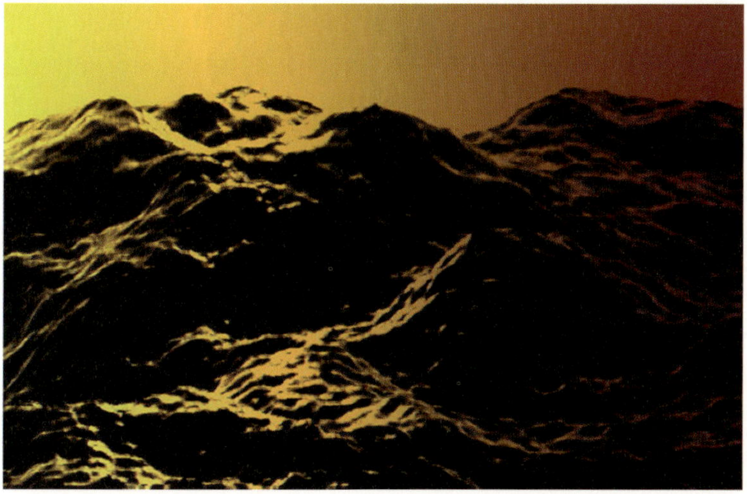

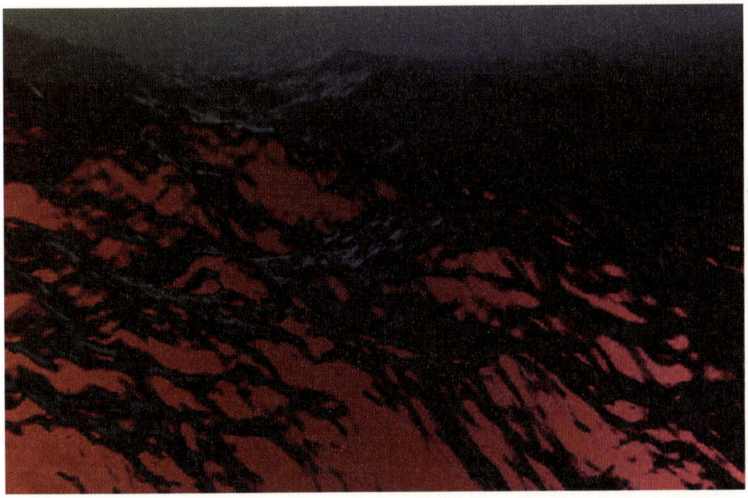

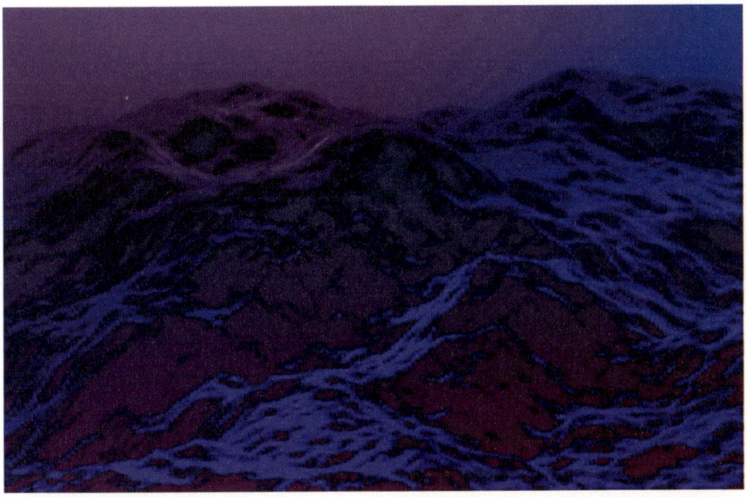

Addresses: Fineartimaging.com/include/images/thumbnails/400/CAR26.jpg, 2006

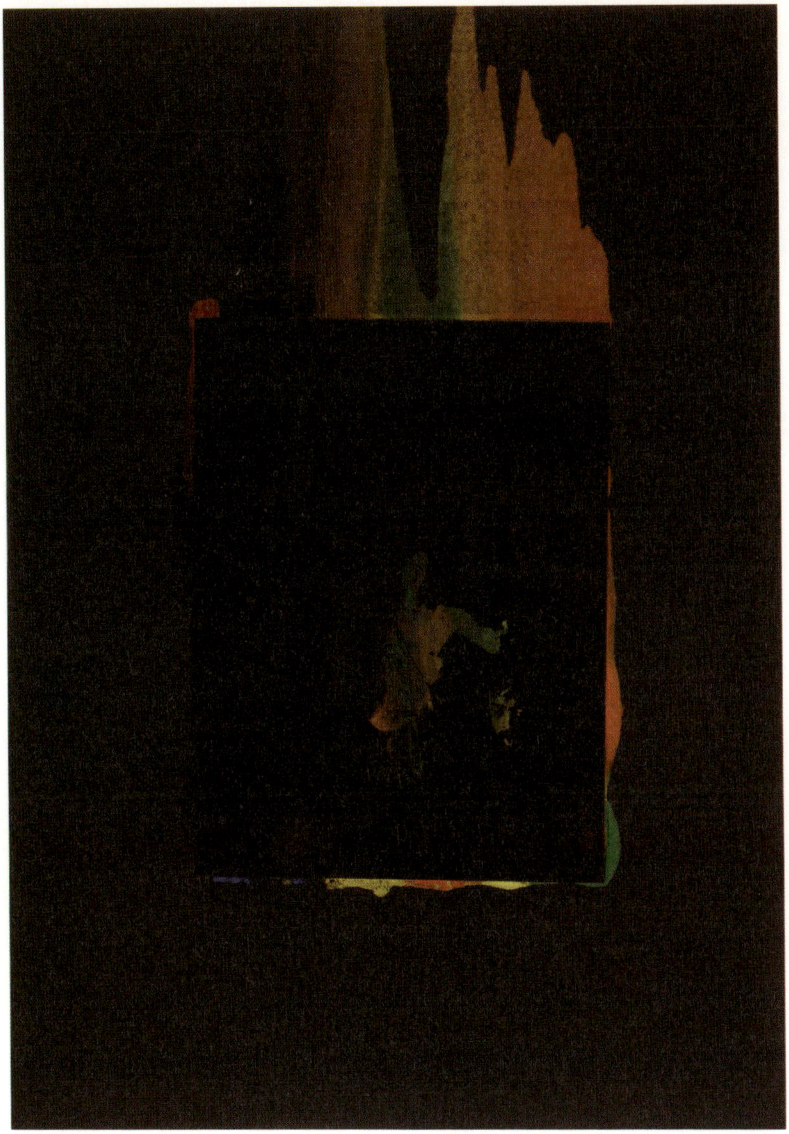

Cultured Bacteria, 2006

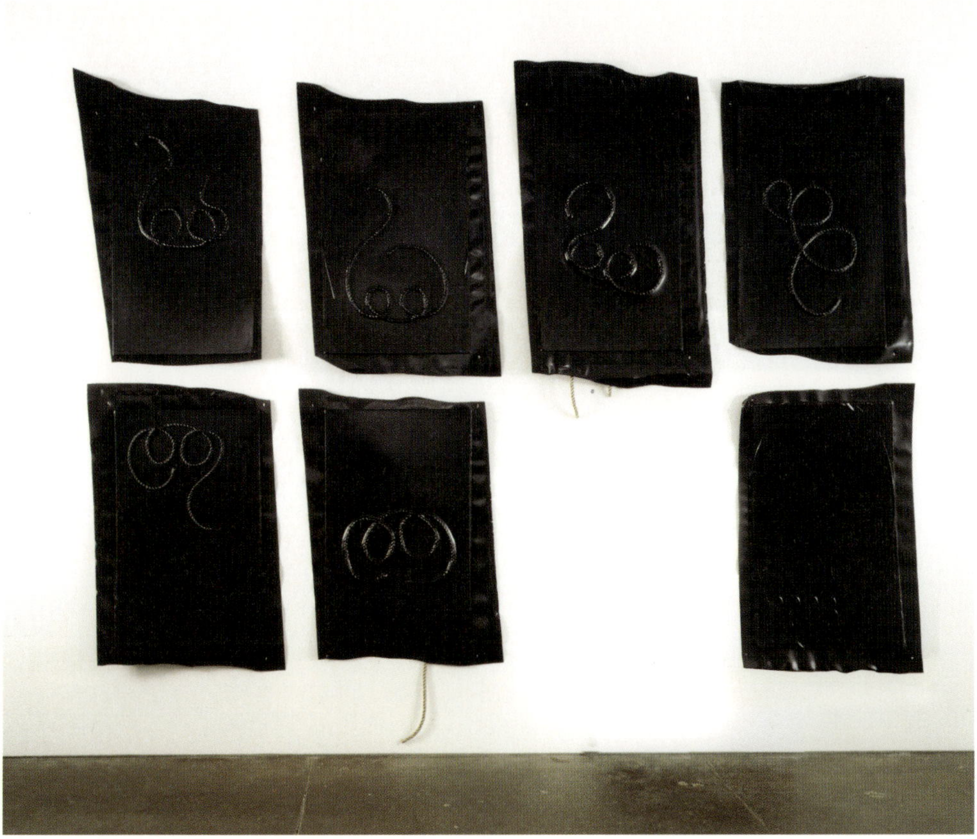

Vintage Bomber, 2006

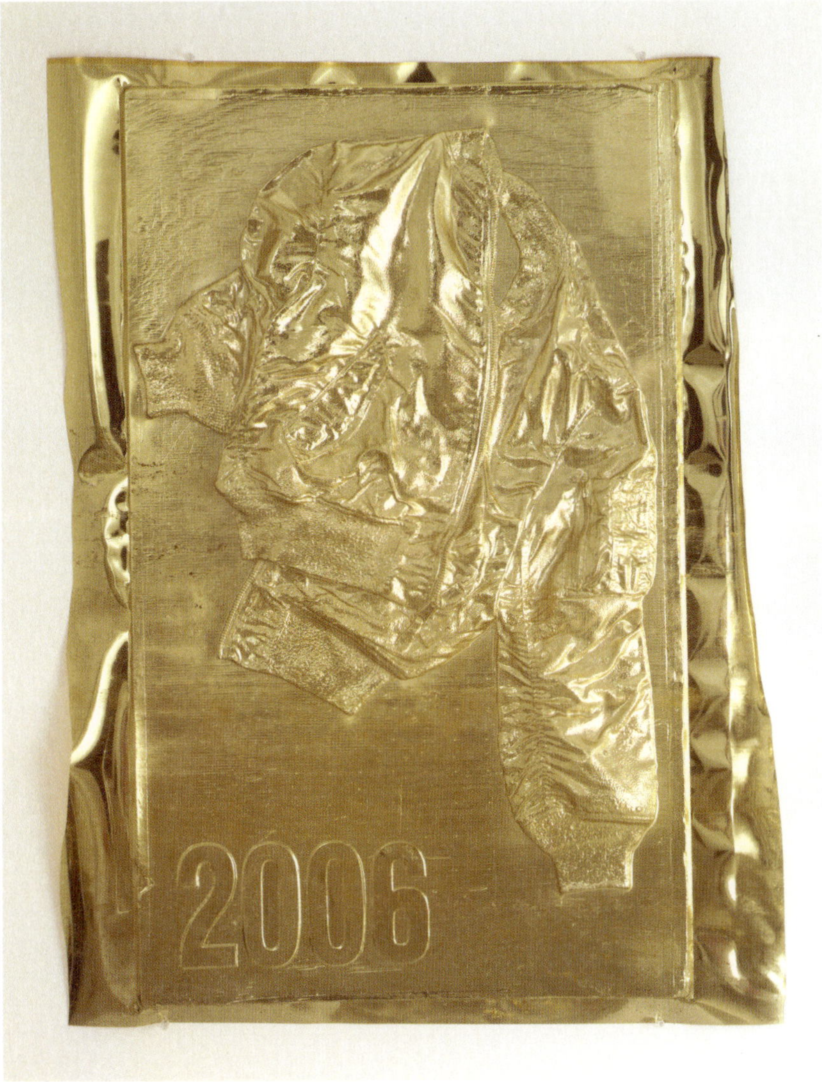
2006

Untitled, 2006

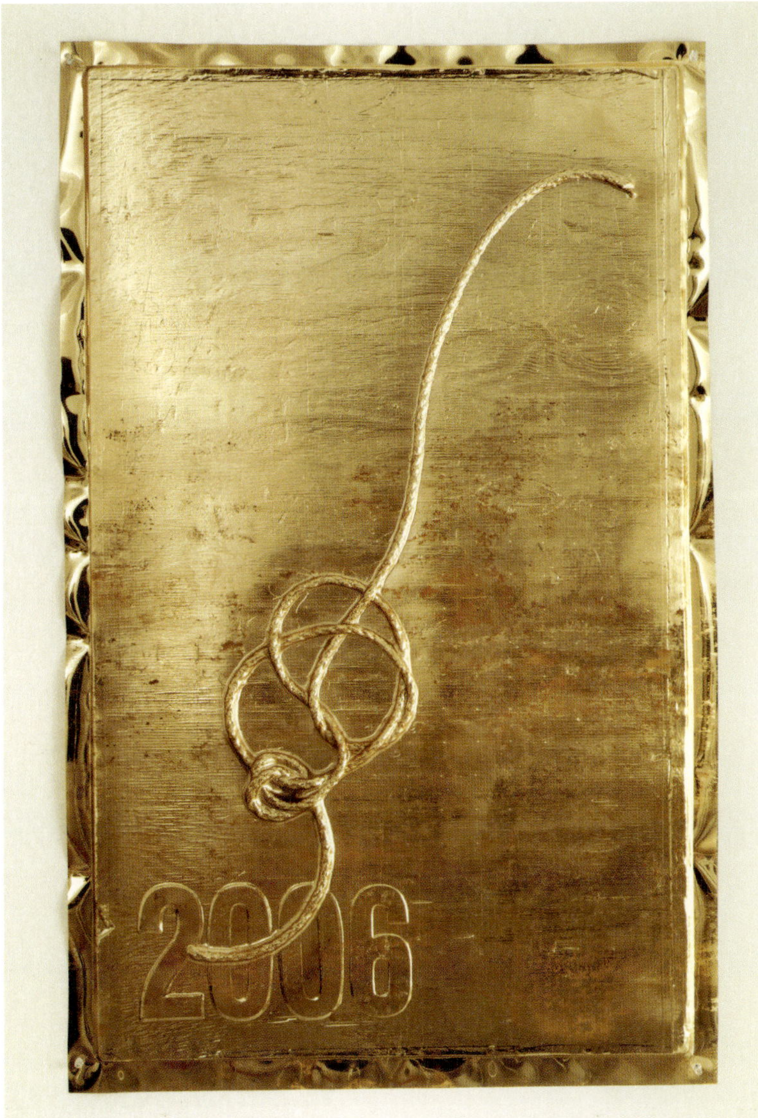
2006

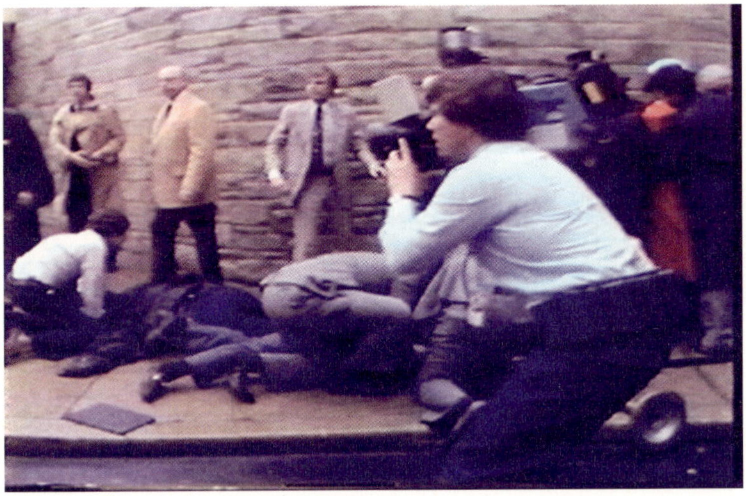

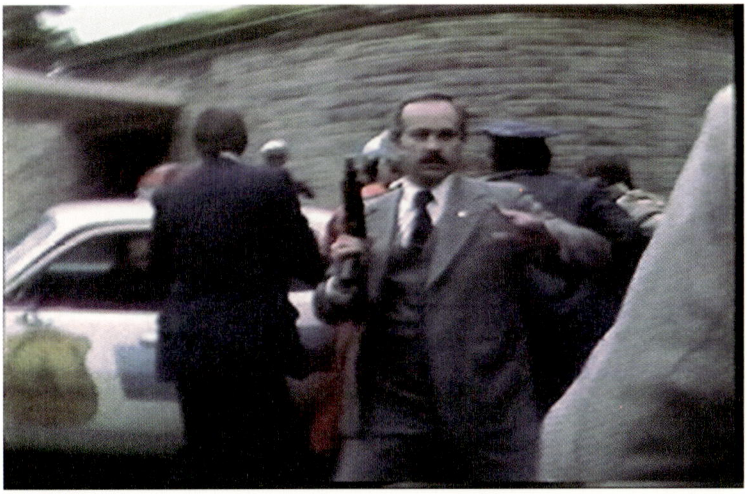

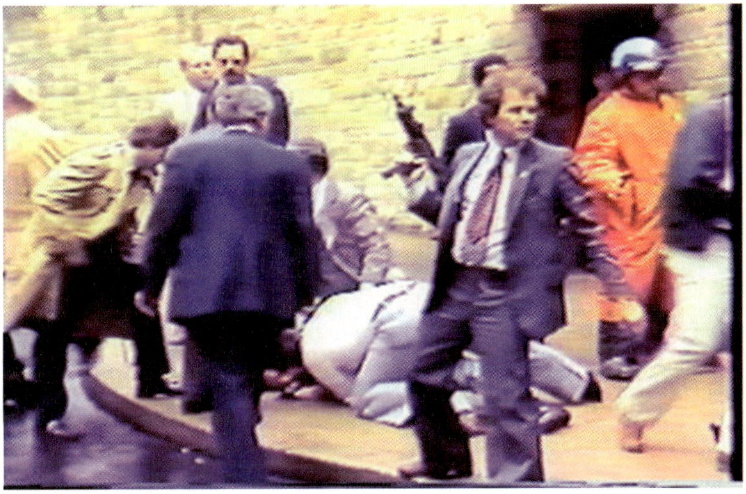

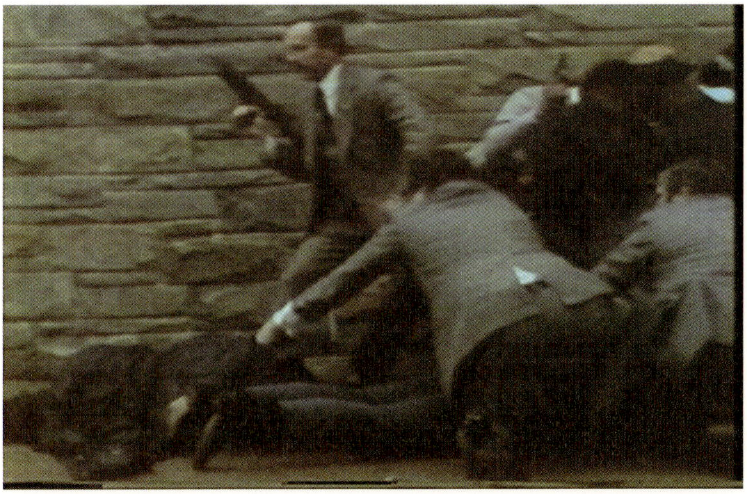

Cheap Wall, 2006

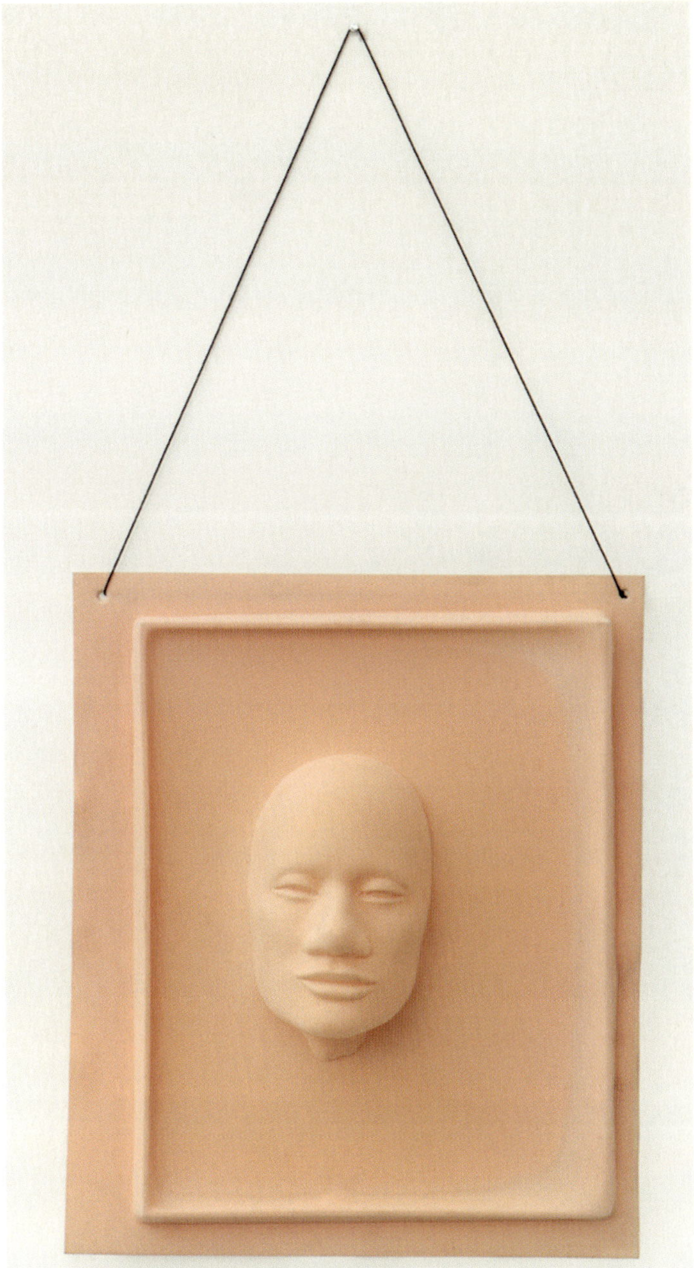

Untitled, 2008

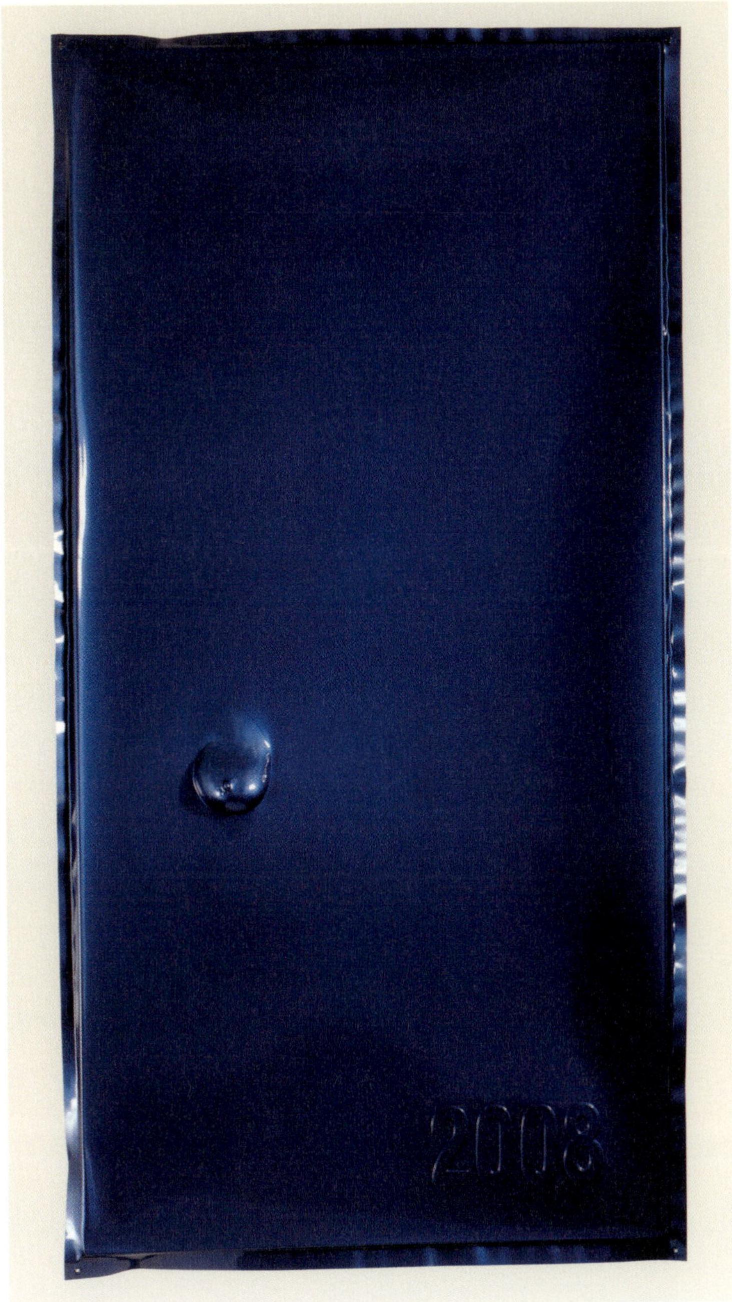
2008

Untitled, 2008

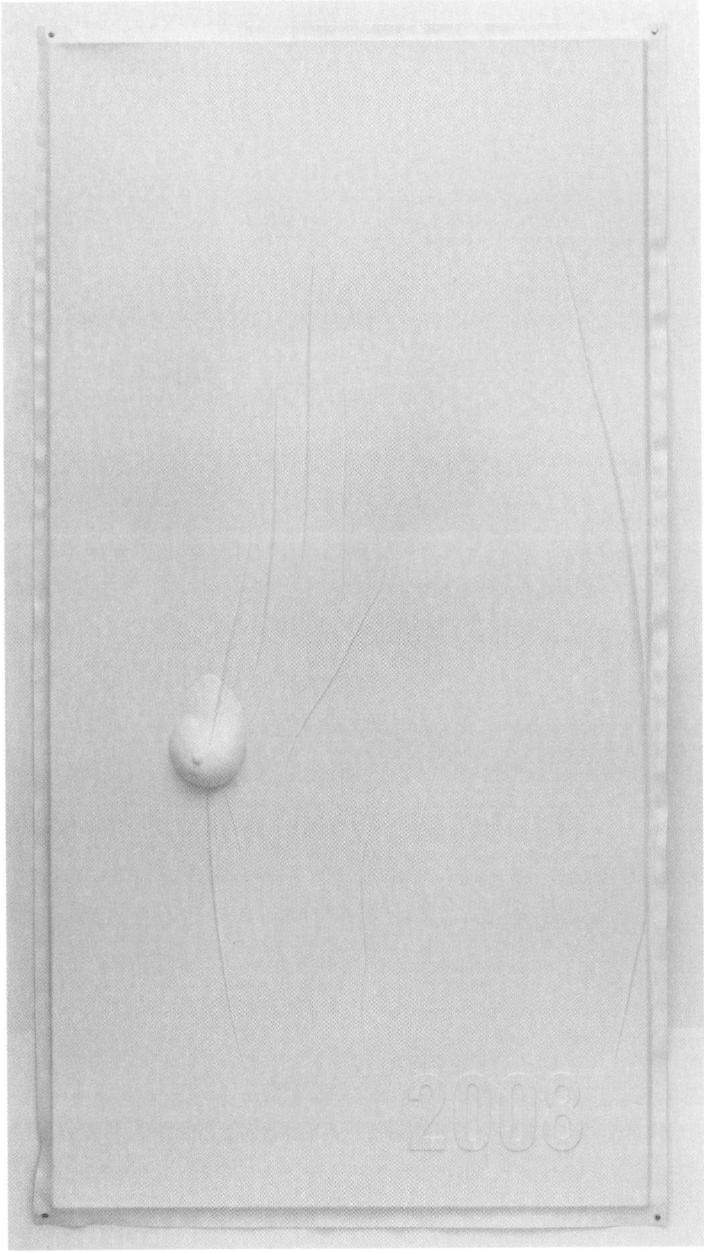
2008

Vintage Bomber, 2008

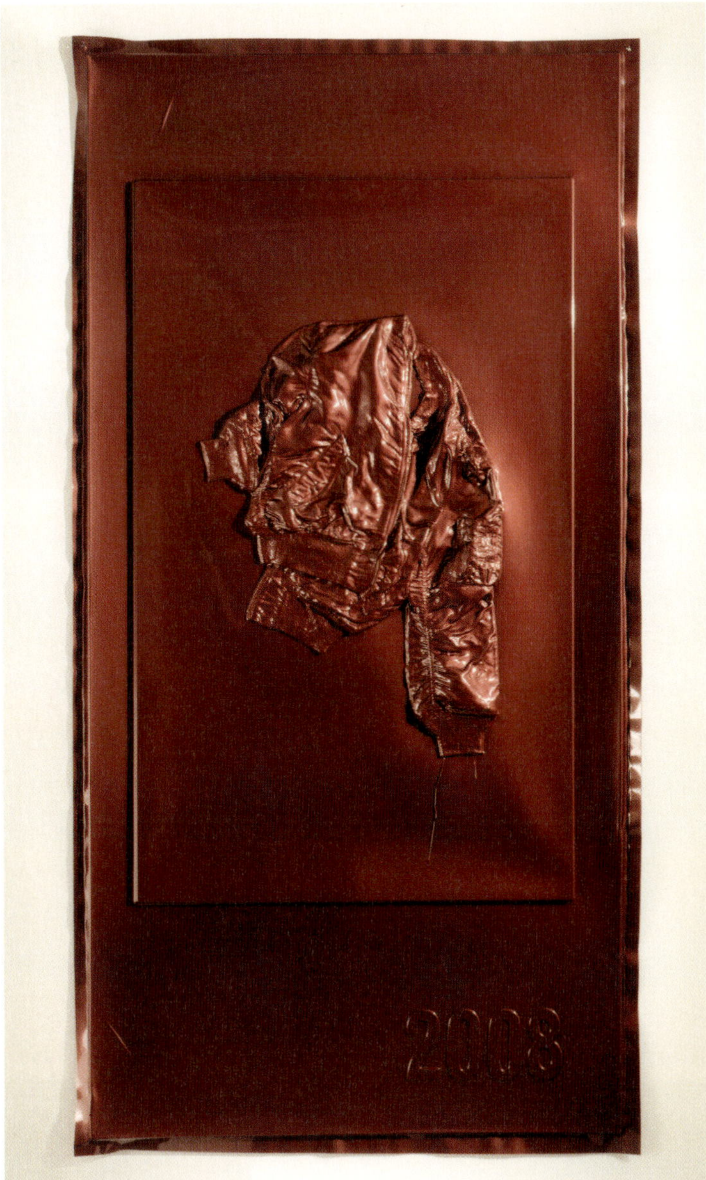
2008

Untitled, 2008

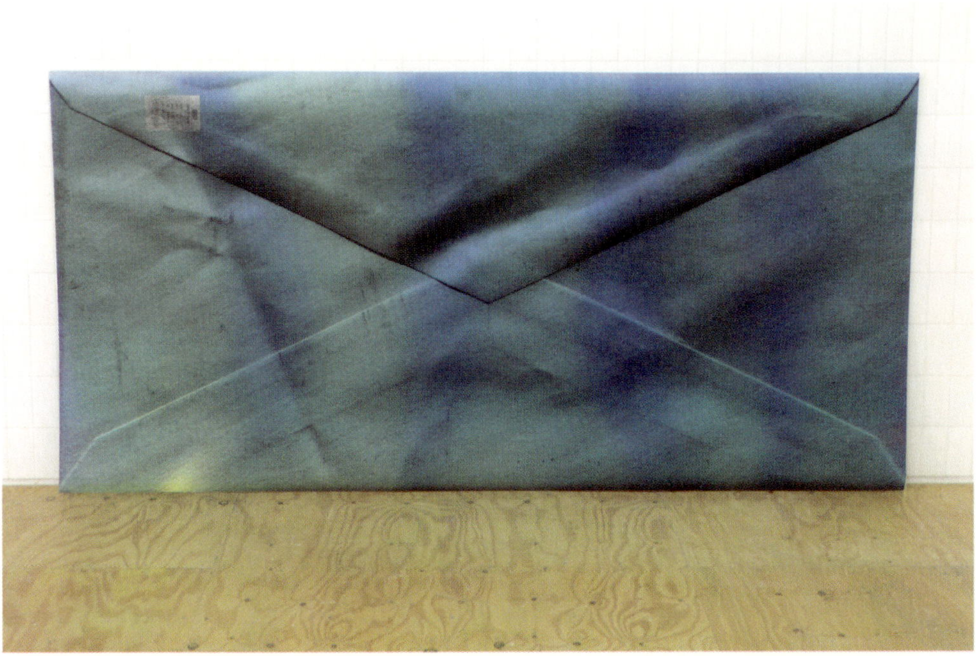

Untitled, 2008

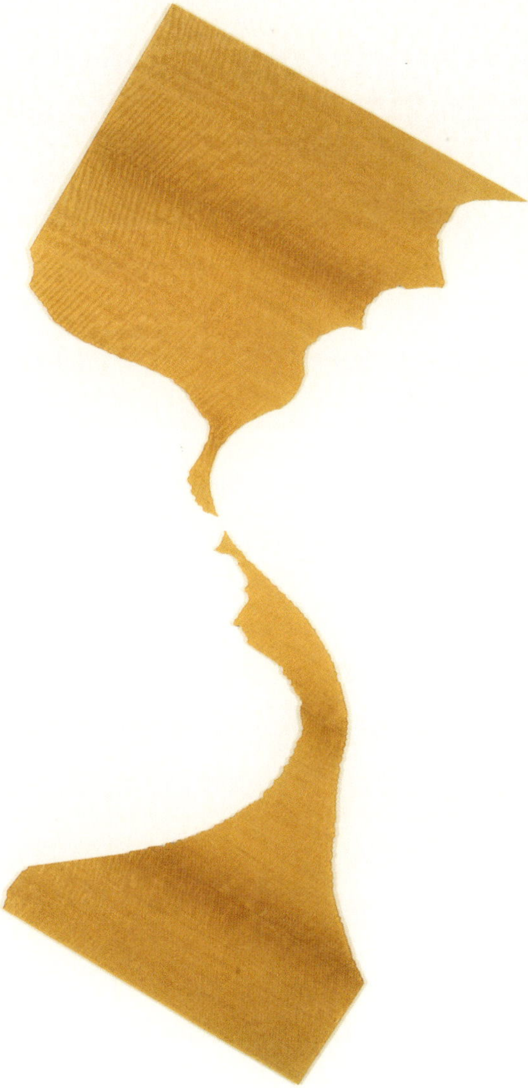

Thing in a Thing, 2011

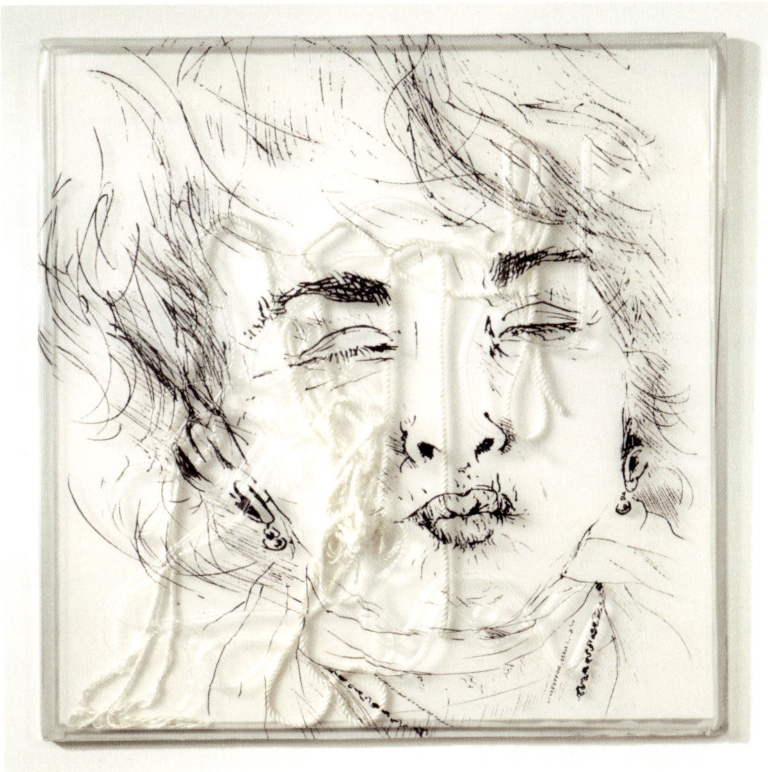

Pencil Legs, 2011

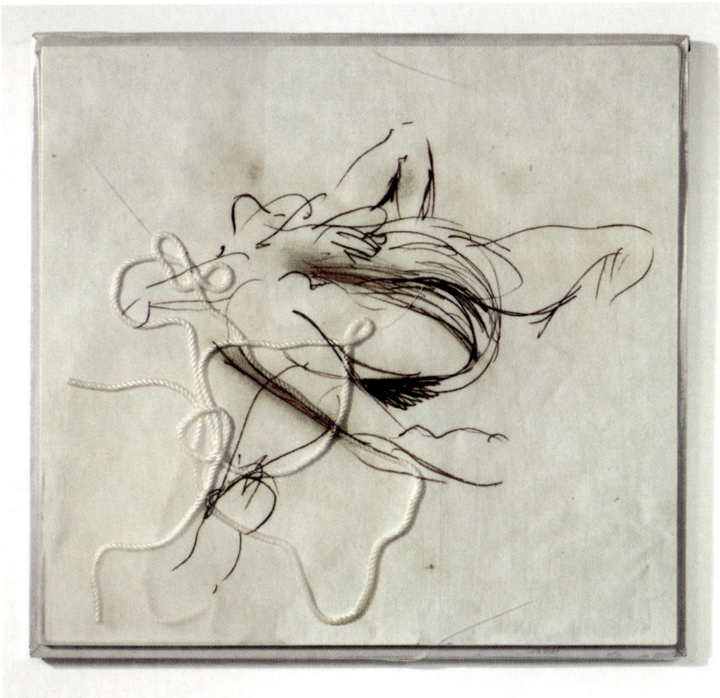

UPTIGHT WORLD

Seth Price

You know how to be cool? First off you don't *be* cool, you *seem* cool. The way you seem cool is to get all quiet and self-assured and apparently at peace with yourself. Not mean, not cold; those are signs of weakness. Just keep your mouth shut, mostly. Another thing, when you *do* say something, say the opposite of what someone else just said, just reverse it. Example: *When we heard they were tossing out all the rules, someone said it would be total anarchy, but my friend said, "No, that's when the Real Rules begin."* It sounds smart, even though it doesn't mean anything. But then you think about it and you start to realize, maybe it does mean something after all.

There's actually a book, a hidden best seller, that tells you dried-up bread crusts how to *seem*. It's basically just rules. Like if someone is like, "What do you think of the new Darkthrone album, it kind of sucks," and you never heard of Darkthrone, you say, "To be honest, and I know this is not a popular opinion, I think it's the best work they've ever done." Just head that shit off at the pass. You flip it, thus planting the seed of uncertainty. When they inquire further you need not explain yourself, you simply go mum, as if explanation—conversation itself—is beneath consideration. Think of it like how you have to cheat to get an actual good haircut: it'll be the coolest, tangled, pushed-back flop-volume, but when you actually comb it straight out it's crap, all ill-cut and raggedy with random strands jagging out. But who cares if you look dorky when you get out of the shower? Actually, on second thought you should say, "I think it's *among* the best work Darkthrone's ever done." Since I know you people hate to be firm or conclusive, even about a bullshit sound bite about shit you don't know shit about.

In summary, if you think about it, all you have to do is flip the common sense. Whatever people typically say or think probably gets interesting if you invert it. If you make a "bad" video, it will probably be more interesting than this pathetic circling around some neurotically formulated concept of what a "good" video could be. If you dress "badly," it will at least be interesting. People on the street will be scoping you out like, "Hmm, that must be the new shit, guess I just don't understand it yet. Sigh." So our line of advice, our *best practices*, would be: "Redundancy, Waste, Perversion, Excess, Don't Try Too Hard, and Do the Bad." But if you want the short version, usually it's enough to simply not make sense.

Understood. My advice is also about words. To pass as an adult you essentially need to master the language used in the medical and legal pro-worlds. Not *master*, really, it's chiefly about attitude, an attitude of mastery and ownership, *seeming*, as you say. But after you get the hang of the basic tonus you're able to attend to the playful and endless matter of manipulating words. For example, in adult world, when someone with that authoritative demeanor scrapes a bit of skin off your forehead with a sharp stick and makes off with it, that's a "biopsy." You got "biopsied." You say, "They did the biopsy; we're waiting for lab results on the blood work." What'd you say your name was? Bopsy? And a guy swiped some ooze off that boo-boo? And now he's in the other room, scratching his head?

Anyway, at a certain point, when you get the hang of this, you can ease into making shit up. A driveway might be a "road approach," or, taking it from the other side of things, a "car approach," or I guess even a "house approach." For example, "Is the property oriented in such a way that there's a good road approach?" Just work it in there as you hash out the deal, no one blinks. Or, "We happen to have three cars, does the property have a car approach on the north side also?" Or, "The house approach is paved with crushed seashells to yield, upon arrival, a pleasantly crankly maritime soupçon." See how authoritative and professional that sounds, like your mind is composed of sharp, interlocking polyhedrons. In fact, I just made that shit up, no one ever heard it before. But it could be some of that new-new. That's how professional lingo gets lab-engineered and virused around.

Alternately, you could maintain that it's a sort of pro-world poetry, that it's pure invention arising from the fundamental need to play, and thus an expression of hope. It's the choice to put your plants in arid soil where good words normally won't grow. And by the way, forget writers who think it's interesting to simply list names of trees and plants, when few readers can be expected to call up images befitting these lovely names: "She stood among swamp oaks, soft maples, tamarack, butternut." Fuck it, that's either poetry or it's a sequential list of entries in a botanist's catalogue. Either way, please leave it alone, craft it right back out of that "pared-to-the-bone" short story.

On the other hand, to get the feeling of reality you do need abundant, senseless detail, which could simply mean lovely words denoting little, i.e., pure evocative sound, i.e., something approaching poetry. And let's face it, most of life consists of standing anxiously in a clearing surrounded by encroaching thickets of shit you don't understand. Like, if you were really standing amongst those particular trees you just mentioned, they don't mean nothing, it would be just more trees. Though if you were ignorant of the names of absolutely *everything* around you, you'd qualify as certifiably insane, and thus incapable of convincing everyone that you're in fact sane. As they drag you off. It's like how with slang sometimes it's better to just not go there. You're not sure what to say, you get all insecure: Yeah, man, we did some *blow*? We were doing *lines*? We blew some *yayo*? Powder? Charlie? Snow? What you do is just say, "Some cocaine." As if you don't even give a fuck enough to complete your. "Some cocaine was consumed." The passive voice. "Heavy cocaine usage last night." Understated, clinical. Everyone respects the hands-off approach with the low-pro glow. Or ditch slang entirely: "Some sex occurred last night." "I'm stepping out; one must needs urinate." Shit flirt with funny. Why? Who know.

Like a marketing exec who pitches a down-market sweetened alcoholic beverage called, say, *Tiané*. Sounds about right. "If we're lucky, in about two years we'll see a lot of babies named *Tiané* born to lower-class urban moms." "Right, right. But maybe we should name it, like, *Liazé*. *L* sounds are trending on the street. Nearly as much as *z* sounds." "But if it's all about *z*, why not *Ziazé*?" "Right. Or we just go with *Zzzzz*." Now that's how you spread influence. Enough influence that you have parents naming kids after your product. And I ain't just talking down-market, neither. . . I mean, if you could actually meet Bob Marley or Bob Dylan, what would you say to them? Like me, you'd probably be curious to know how they feel about their Christian names being slapped on a few thousand male babies. "When we get there tonight, don't forget to ask if Marley and Dylan got into Gifted & Talented." On the one hand, a pre-tarnished skull ring, on the other, a Tribeca-flavored edible undergarment. You people just consume and consume and consume, and then you're sick and must stop and vomit it all up for the next meal.

But I don't agree. Because that's actually how a person makes stuff. It's not from some position of withdrawal or purity, rather the opposite. What do we like? Josef Frank textiles, Nathalie Du Pasquier jewelry, clothes by Paul Harnden, Zen Buddhism, but not mainstream Buddhism, anything by Bach, anything by Kafka. I could go on. As for the pre-tarnished–jewelry metaphor, do you honestly feel that "back in the eighties" men were still men, women were women, the mainstream was the mainstream, and the underground was the underground? That all the barriers were still in place, *but in a productive way*, and now we're tossing out all the rules? I mean to say, is it genuinely the fault of the nineties? The truth is that just because you lived through a period or listened to its music when it was new or wore the styles of that age, this means precious little. You possess no claim to any of it, no more than we who come later to heft it and put it under a light and study these artifacts with disinterest. It may be better to approach everything as a researcher. You wore dolman-sleeved jackets? You liked Run-DMC in 1983 and Royal Trux in 1993? Who gives a shit? You moved on and rejected it, or it rejected you. I choose it consciously, I own it more than you ever did. Because we take these inconsequential leavings and background noise and fuck them into weapons. We'll take the wretched loop playing while you're on hold with your bank and stutter it into a sensation. We like things broken down and infirm. The more amateur the better. Although it's not that they are "broken," it's that they never worked properly in the first place. We once set out to spray a Mercedes sign on the wall but mistakenly made a peace sign. The spray paint was applied too thickly and kind of dripped down to fill in the missing line segment; it happened after we'd already left the scene. And fuck mid-century Modernism, shit's boring. We like the thirties for furniture. Also the nineties. We appreciate Memphis, of course, but now that house is too crowded. Whoever was building furniture when the towers fell, seek out that person and sink your investment. We "kind of hate" Apple, but we use it anyway. Look, by the time you're seven you basically know what your limits are: you're not Italian, but you *are* tall and lovely; you're not Tom Cruise—who's tiny and anxious-making—but who cares, these days no one cares about celebrities. How many freaking movie stars we down to, now, Will Smith? Fucking ghost town over there. Ditch that twentieth-century shit, we rather make micro-hallucinations and jury-rigged imitation. Drop your interest in film, photography, montage, collage, fragments, heterogeneity, speed—in a word, *modernity*, plus the hysterical love of modernity you've daubed with prefixes like *post-* and *super-* and *hyper-*. Film as a metaphor is done, along with all those artworks and experimental fictions that used film as a structuring or narrative device, or that allude to jump cuts, establishing shots, montage, zooms and pans, frames per second, deep focus, seething grain. Or later, starting in the eighties, all those people who got excited about video as metaphor: test patterns, cathode rays lighting up the dark, vertical holds and densities of broadcast snow, horizontal scan lines stacked like noir window blinds, everyone living in a realm flickering, unstable, and staticky, close to the edit, in the video store aisles, in the erotic insertion of a tape into a hole in a unit. Whether on film or on video, movies are essentially a boring, short-lived historical flash, just signal to noise.

The twist is that cinema has a twin, born and raised right alongside: The Story. In your fixation on moving images you're like those fiction writers clinging to this corny-ass idea of literature as human interest: Uhhh, it is sweeping, even as it is a collection of lapidary "set pieces," it surveys modern history as well as our little moment, it addresses individual psychology plus the swamp of family, it respects passion and feeling, and it is fundamentally humorous, since we see humor as a vital means of bringing people together, of easing the common burden of our "humanity," plus an absurdist bite in reality's squat neck. But just because you suck doesn't mean you're a vampire. To all you out there crafting set pieces about people who love and fight, our struggles and hopes, how petty and silly and human we are with our *frailty*, a quality we worship, disdain, coddle, and above all *leverage*: well, we don't feel much like laughing or crying, particularly.

In that case, you need to ditch all those dreams that snuck in uninvited, smuggled in the crack between movies and stories. Example: there is a dream specific to the twentieth century, and it is peddled by movies and books and advertisements, and it describes the lovely little town that conceals evil or chaos "beneath its placid surface." Establishing shot: a panoramic, sweeping pan of an LA Valley scene, low dry hills lined with ranch houses, kids on bikes tracing lazy loop-de-loops; or, alternately, a calm and steady zoom high over leafy East Coast suburbs in autumn, a maroon station wagon slowing to round a corner and pass from sight, Victorian wood-frame houses under maples rustling in the wind: winter's coming. Which we already know, because it's a twentieth-century picture, it's thoroughly uptight about the "what lies beneath" thing. Which petered out some time in the nineties. And what replaced it? That's the question of today.

What? You talking about the nineties? Furniture is one thing, but what about all those guys who follow an aesthetic credo that has them looking one step from homelessness, or grad school at least: frayed button-downs, mussed hair, scuffed non–Black Person sneakers, and no logos at all, unless they're total non sequiturs (e.g., a tee announcing "Vidal Sassoon," admittedly an amusing name). Dried-up bread crusts from the indie-rock era. Fine, but you're in your forties and fifties now! Get some effing dignity, man. That's the thing about men's fashion, it's chiefly about dignity. Women can play the coquette, but for men, straight or gay, the chief thing is dignity. You understand that, you can make a pile of money.

Right, but the thing about decades. You're still fairly young. When you first learn about decades as a structuring idea you're quite small, and ten years seems like a long time. The problem is that this casual understanding of decades stays with you far longer than it has any right to. By the time you're poised at what the ancients called "the midpoint of life"—i.e., your thirties—your experience of time has matured, and you should have come to understand that ten years is nothing, that this division of the century into decades is silliness, that the endless shambolic sliding of trends, historical moments, and cultural eras resembles only the behavior of ungainly amounts of refuse as a container is tipped over to send its contents slithering and slipping over and around themselves and into the next container, leaving greasy muck everywhere.

Yes, but occasionally you have to take out the garbage. What do I really know about life after World War II? I mean, I'll tell you what. Okay, "Postwar Era." Everyone says everything changed. What really changed is that in the fifties people had pretty tight haircuts. Shit was tight and slicked out. But kind of naïve? I don't know if that was coming out of the Great Depression, some kind of scarcity/rationalism issue, or more from the militarization of a whole society or whole generation, i.e., an uptight optic. Or what. Because most guys had longer hair than that, even just thirty or forty years earlier. History's so schizo. But by the end of the sixties everyone had just went completely the other way, crazy-long hair, just "stop cutting, stop cutting," but also stop combing, stop grooming, stop using soap. Probably because more people had color TV, and the movies were into kids all of a sudden, and that whole discovery of older people having short hair, you know, it was a rejection of uptightness that was actually itself mad uptight. Do you know what I mean? So by the end of the seventies hair got a little less shaggy and long, or at least less long, but they were still into the natural vibe; even if it wasn't quite as long, it got, like, super-styled, you were taking a long time to make it look like your hair was natural and had no product or anything, but it was all puffed out and kind of dry, kind of blow-dried, because if it was *really* natural it would get all ratty, and all nasty with sebum, and you didn't want that. Then in the eighties they *really* discovered product, or maybe the dudes who make product had some serious brainstorms to, like, rescue us from that fifties slicked-out thing. Because eighties haircuts got crazy severe, kind of like fifties haircuts that finally got fuck-you blood, like they saw their dad knifed, by their mom, and they got sent to a foster home, and learned to, you know, keep a lookout. No, I'm just playing. But really, if you were an art school girl in the eighties, you were definitely thinking about the fifties, you had a little leather biker jacket and cat eye glasses and suede creepers. Which would all live in the back of the closet until well after your first baby. And then in the nineties people go back to kind of more scruffed-out styles, like dudes in bands getting back into long hair and the ratty look, but now they had that serious product lust in their blood, and there is just absolutely no putting that genie back in the bottle. And in the two-thousands people started getting creative, like: now that we found gel, what are we going to do about it? Suddenly you could wake up to the reality of bangs. My personal gripe is that so many dudes with long hair have the same retarded non-style, which apparently arises from a belief that long hair means granting every strand an equal opportunity to reach its full potential. It's thick, it's shapeless, it's falling to the shoulders, and there it gets chopped. It looks like a supposedly urban-minimal throw rug that, through factory error, was woven from polar fleece. Memo to guys: there's a reason women have a culture of salons, stylists, and products: we have to deal with all this hair! Get it together, guys, get it taken care of professionally. Come on. How many products in your hair, motherfucker? You should have three: a leave-in candy, a pomade, and a silk groom. Plus that stuff on your scalp for the dandruff, sebum, whatever it is.

But you young adults are often slightly out of focus, as if your accumulated lack of consideration for or ignorance of all the lives open to you has clouded your mien. Dim little stars, glimpsed only from the side. All u earnest people who decry the transformations money has wrought on this town (a city changing before our eyes, developers remaking us in the image of health and safety, guard the memory of all that is lost!) have no understanding of what's been gained, and not in the positivist terms developers and politicians use, but in terms of all the oddball approaches to life that real people rustle up in the face of massive body blows. To their lifestyles. Get used to it, it's here, by all means organize to combat the next onslaught, but stop pining for what you've lost, it demeans all the things that we down here have wrested from the wreckage.

Yes, but to take that urban-gentrification image to the next level, what you're talking about is exactly the situation of being a young person today, poking your head out of the muck and getting a sack of muck in the face. That's right. Motherfucker, it's all about the youth. You hate the young, and it's only because they will die long after you, it's obvious. Experience only makes people duller and more depleted and more tired, not wiser. As we slowly morph into those who make a virtue of failure by calling it a sign of resistance.

So, in closing, here's a little game we play. You just add "if you're young" to any clichéd lyric or advertising tagline, and thereby derive the true, hidden sense.

Night time is the right time (if you're young)
Life is a bowl of cherries (if you're young)
Just do it (if you're young)
Be all you can be (if you're young)

I see your humor. And I raise you one. For we prefer to play another, related game.

Life is a highway (unless you're old)
Think different (unless you're old)
A diamond is forever (unless you're old)
A mind is a terrible thing to waste (unless you're old)

Oh yeah, that be so funny, that be totally working!

Yeah, it be like something I could sell to a real stand-up guy! I mean, a stand-up comedy guy.

No, aiming higher, maybe: something to sell to a late-night talk show host?

Yeah, well, speaking of time. We're writing a book called either *The Day Before Tomorrow* or *The Day After Yesterday*. We can't decide which.

Oh, that's so funny, because our new book is called just *Today*.

LIST OF WORKS

Untitled Film/Right, 2006
16 mm film, silent
Duration: 14 min.
Edition 1/5

Addresses: Fineartimaging.com/include/images/thumb-nails/400/CAR26.jpg, 2006
Etching and oil monoprint on Arches paper
113 x 76.5 cm

Cultured Bacteria, 2006
Ropes, vacuum-formed high-impact polystyrene
Seven parts, each approx. 152.4 x 86.3 cm, overall approx. 355.6 x 381 cm
Unique

Vintage Bomber, 2006
Vacuum-formed high-impact polystyrene
121.9 x 86.4 cm
Unique

Untitled, 2006
Vacuum-formed high-impact polystyrene over rope knot
121.9 x 74.9 cm
Unique

COPYRIGHT 2006 SETH PRICE, Seth Price, 2006
Video of CBS and ABC raw news footage with variably altered color and speed, silent
Duration: 12:48 min.
Edition 1/5 + 1AP

Cheap Wall, 2006
Vacuum-formed high-impact polystyrene
52 x 42 x 10 cm
Unique

Untitled, 2008
Vacuum-formed high-impact polystyrene and synthetic enamel
243.8 x 121.9 cm
Unique

Untitled, 2008
Vacuum-formed high-impact polystyrene
244 x 122 cm

Vintage Bomber, 2008
Vacuum-formed high-impact polystyrene and synthetic enamel
243.8 x 121.9 cm
Unique

Untitled, 2008
UV-cured inkjet on protective safety film over mirrored iridescent acrylic
1.21 x 2.43 m
Unique

Untitled, 2008
Fiddleback iroko wood and diamond acrylic
238.8 x 142.2 cm
Unique

Thing in a Thing, 2011
UV-cured inkjet on PETG vacuum-formed over rope
114.3 x 118.1 cm

Pencil Legs, 2011
UV-cured inkjet and enamel on PETG vacuum-formed over rope
114.3 x 118.1 cm

ARTIST BIO

Seth Price was born in Palestine in 1973. His work investigates the dissemination and valuation of art in a consumerist culture. Focusing on new media dispersion methods that aim to make his own and others' work universally accessible, Price's varied works include sculptures, video, paintings, books, prints, music and music videos, vacuum-formed reliefs, and even a clothing line, which he designed in collaboration with designer Tim Hamilton.

Price has mounted solo exhibitions at institutions including the Museo d'Arte Moderna in Bologna, Italy (2009); Kunsthalle Zürich, Switzerland (2008); Kölnischer Kunstverein, Cologne, Germany (2008); and Reena Spaulings Fine Art, New York (2006). He has shown his work in group exhibitions including *The System of Objects* at the DESTE Foundation for Contemporary Art, Athens, Greece (2013); *dOCUMENTA (13)*, Kassel, Germany (2012); *ILLUMInations* at the Venice Biennale, Italy (2011); the 8th Gwangju Biennale, Korea (2010); the fourth Tate Triennial at Tate Britain, London, England (2009); *A Guest + A Host = A Ghost* at the DESTE Foundation for Contemporary Art (2009); *Seth Price/Kelly Walker/Continuous Project* at Modern Art Oxford, England (2007); and the 2002 and 2008 Whitney Biennials at the Whitney Museum of American Art, New York. Price lives and works in New York City.

AUTHOR BIO

Chris Wiley is an artist, writer, and curator based in New York and Los Angeles. As a writer, he is a regular contributor to *Frieze*, *Artforum*.com, and *Kaleidoscope* magazine, where he is an editor-at-large. He has contributed texts and essays for numerous exhibitions and catalogs at the New Museum of Contemporary Art in New York, the 8th Gwangju Biennale, Korea, and the 55th Venice Biennale.

As a curator, he has collaborated and advised on several exhibitions at the New Museum of Contemporary Art, including *Ghosts in the Machine* (2012), *Ostalgia* (2011), *The Generational: Younger Than Jesus* (2009) and *After Nature* (2008). He served as the assistant curator on the 8th Gwangju Biennale and as head writer and advisor on the 55th Venice Biennale. In 2012, he curated *Towards A Warm Math* at On Stellar Rays in New York. As an artist, he has had solo exhibitions at MoMA PS1 (2014), Nicelle Beauchene Gallery, New York (2012), and the University of the Arts, Philadelphia (2007).

I am thankful to Seth Price for his work and for his sophisticated views on art, which continue to extend my understanding of what art can be and where it can be found. I am especially happy that we are publishing a new text by Seth that has never been published before. Thank you to Chris Wiley, whose essay illuminates Seth's work by following it in all its metamorphoses and digressions. Thanks to Massimiliano Gioni for his surprising juxtapositions of artists and writers in the *2000 Words* series. A great thank you to Karen Marta and Sue Medlicott for another great volume, carefully edited and produced. And special thanks to Brendan Dugan for his consistently refreshing vision and design.

—Dakis Joannou

Seth Price
2000 Words

Commissioning Editor: Massimiliano Gioni
Editor: Karen Marta
Design: An Art Service
Editorial Assistant: Quinn Lewington
Coordinators: Regina Alivisatos and Dustin Cosentino
Registrar: Natasha Polymeropoulos
Copy Editors: Miles Champion and Grace Moss
Production: The Production Department

Published by:
The DESTE Foundation for Contemporary Art
Filellinon 11 & Em. Pappa St.
N. Ionia 142 34, Athens
www.deste.gr

Cover: Seth Price, *Untitled*, 2008
Thank you to Kat Parker and Ko Sadakuni at Petzel Gallery, New York, and Makiko Ushiba

Distributed in the Americas by:
ARTBOOK | D.A.P.
155 Sixth Avenue, 2nd Floor
New York, NY 10013
www.artbook.com

Distributed in Europe by:
Buchhandlung Walther König
Ehrenstrasse 4
50672 Köln
www.buchhandlung-walther-koenig.de

Printed in Greece by Alta Grafico S.A. Printing and Graphic Arts

ISBN: 978-618-5039-07-3